To Shelby -

Always let your words flow
? your dreams soar! You are
beautiful!

Leslie Chiappell

painted toes

painted toes

Leslie Chiappetti

iUniverse, Inc.
New York Lincoln Shanghai

painted toes

Copyright © 2005 by Leslie Rosenberg Chiappetti

iUniverse books may be ordered through booksellers or by contacting:

iUniverse
2021 Pine Lake Road, Suite 100
Lincoln, NE 68512
www.iuniverse.com
1-800-Authors (1-800-288-4677)

ISBN-13: 978-0-595-33901-3 (pbk)
ISBN-13: 978-0-595-67028-4 (cloth)
ISBN-13: 978-0-595-78686-2 (ebk)
ISBN-10: 0-595-33901-8 (pbk)
ISBN-10: 0-595-67028-8 (cloth)
ISBN-10: 0-595-78686-3 (ebk)

Printed in the United States of America

This book is dedicated to those who believe.

Contents

Introduction xi

The Rainbow 1

Painted Toes 2

Layers 3

Masterpiece 4

I Believe 5

Paintbrush 6

Fireworks 7

Jazz 8

Ancient Clay 9

Evolution 10

The Reason 11

The Real Me 12

Tinges of Blue 13

Hanging On 14

Giving Up 15

Waves 16

Nobody 17

Getting Through 18

War Zone 19

So Far Away 20

Unneeded 21

Disappointing Breeze 22

Hypnotized 23

Another Door 24

Living in My House 25

I Don't Have the Strength 26

Naked 27

Flashes of Red 28

In My Head 29

Sex 30

Bonfire 31

Entranced 32

Senses 33

Yin Yang 35

My Reality 36

Goodnight 37

Lord, Help Me 38

Creamy White 39

Theirs 40

Waiting for Grace 41

Our Wedding 42

The Promise 43

Leo 44

Saffron 45

Serenity 46

It's Just the Way You Are 47

But I Can 48

In Your Head 49

Sail With Me *50*

It's You *51*

In an Instant *52*

My Joy *53*

Beiges and Browns 54

Ecosystem *55*

Disengaged *56*

Building a Home *57*

Distraction *58*

Time *59*

Marathon *60*

Bath *62*

Examination *63*

The Mountain *64*

Standing Outside *65*

For You *66*

Shades of Gray 68

Chasing the Light *69*

The Anatomy of Needing *70*

Awaken *71*

Secrets *72*

Day Dreaming *73*

Strange Existence *74*

Waiting *75*

Breaking the Cycle *76*

18 . . . . *77*

Changing Hues 79

Soul Sister *80*

First Steps *81*

Psychic Thoughts *82*

Lying in Bed *83*

Sensibility *84*

Quilt *85*

Time to Rest *86*

Innocence *87*

Makeupping *88*

A Sign *89*

First Breath *90*

His God Within *91*

He Wasn't the One *92*

Introduction

painted toes are poems I have created over the last 15 years. Each color represents a common thread to which we all can relate. And, when choosing a color to paint my toes, I always find great pleasure in taking my time, picking each bottle up, shaking it, and feeling its mood before I settle in with just one. But the result is a direct connection to my heart.

My poems were always written to tell someone how I truly felt at that moment—my emotions at the core level. I needed to express it, whether it was the highest level of passion or the depths of longing. I have left hand-written poems on the night stand, send them in emails and framed them in gaudy, glass frames. They are for my husband, my daughter, my son and my friends.

painted toes is the narrator inside a woman's mind and the glow about her when she knows her toes are exactly the way she wants them to be.

The Rainbow

Painted Toes

Most summer days
you can see them.
My expression,
my reality
when you look down
at my toes.
An azure glaze
telling my enigmatic
need for a different hue.
In the Fall,
it's a bit hidden
but they are there,
a cherry luster to
balance out my heart.
Harsh breezes blow
as I revel in the fresh
coat of paint I
slowly streaked and
dabbed away the drips.
I watch out the window
for tender blades of grass
to appear
as I shake off my shoes
to walk down the block
and celebrate
my painted toes.

Layers

Dimensions
create themselves.
Adding a new layer
to a solid foundation.
Rainbow hues and
silky textures
wind around
diamond hard columns.
Each minute
my soul evolves
as does my love
for you.
Never dormant
ever piecing together
an endless moment,
a weightless existence,
a definite future.

Masterpiece

My dawn
is a mixture of gold
and mellow blue.
I see the sun
as an evil ally
forcing me to rise
and continue.
Hot reds and
refrigerator greens
merging into
a tale of new visions
resulting from
crashing adolescent dreams.
Then I see you.
Its creamy smooth,
a warm blanket
not just covering
but sealing the edges
of my wound.
Complete blindness
has become a masterpiece
of enlightenment.
A palate has been
created from
an apparition of passion.

I Believe

Innate
and well rounded.
The sense was not always
apparent on the surface.
Faith became a friend
as logic decided to
exit stage left.

Paintbrush

Colliding colors
in a palate we created
run together to blend
a portrait of exploding desire.
I begin the sketch from
memory and fill
in lines of character
produced from voices,
photos and perception.
The pictures take form-
live and breathe
each moment we
perpetuate their life
with our love.

Fireworks

A crack of thunder,
sizzling streamers of light
shoot green and gold-
physical relief
with each caress of your voice.
The fingers of fire
seem to fall back into
my brain and get in line
behind hundreds of rustling
ideas waiting to be released.
Memories roll on a movie
screen behind my eyes
rewinding the beginning
and rewarding those
who purchased tickets
to be here.
The hero arrives
to sweep the fair maiden
away as the train approaches
narrowly escaping death.
As the sun sets
their kiss is emphasized
by the blazing fireworks
over their heads.

Jazz

Swaying to the music,
eyes closed,
legs and arms entwined.
Sighing into myself
as my ears fill
with breath and saxophone.
I am unaware of the low
hum of people around us
at tables with lovers.
With your arms wrapped tight,
I keep moving and praying
for this song to never end.

Ancient Clay

I come to you
naked and unadorned
free from
consequential shackles,
weakness that drained
my blood.
You have filled me with
warm, flowing honey,
glistening on my forehead
in a field of sunflowers
pouring into your mouth
as we make love.
I come to you
a woman.
Needing nothing
but our inspiration,
the mortar that holds
ancient clay-
a home to families
bringing us to that place.
Our history.
Our future.

Evolution

How do you explain
that a year has been centuries,
a moment is an hour,
and a kiss brings up the sun.
I have met my
inspirational match as
endless moments reveal
the fury of passion.
Your simplistic values
have changed me
from tiny pieces of uncertainty
to a woman of conviction
with the heart that holds
your life,
your love,
and one day, your child.
It is why nothing grants me
the will to wander.

The Reason

I want to write
to take it away.
I need these words
to relieve me,
fill me with incontestable joy.
The urgency grows
and my fingers itch.
My eyes dart
around the page.
I wait for the next
line to emerge.
When that one
doesn't satiate,
I continue.
I sip my coffee
and feel the heavy
moments tick and
pass with infinite presence.

The Real Me

It hit me.
A realization
beyond words,
sound, thought.
It was a
slow smile
as my lips reacted
to the vibration
of my heart.
Inconceivable to many,
unconventional
as a moral dilemma.
It exists as
a pure formation.
Accept me,
oh Lord,
help me to love again.
Guide me
to give what I know
to be the soul
I have fought
to uncover.

Tinges of Blue

Hanging On

Fighting invisible monsters.
Flailing out at the air
around me.
Still knowing the spirits
whisper knowledge
into my brain.
I listen intently.
I walk away from validity.
Voices clearly heard
above the rest
soothe and prod.
I shake my head
in categorical fear.
The demons sit quietly
listening to my logic
and decide to retire
for the day.
Comfort comes as
a warm breeze from
the east.
Angels carry the message
carefully with conviction.

Giving Up

I see through you.
Moving parts,
deceptive actions,
thinking you will
move one way
and you move the other.
Words bind me
as I watch
your bare bones
do a selfish dance.
Time passes quickly
as you try to
get me to join you.
But I don't.
My hands stay in my lap
and my shoes
under the bed.

Waves

On a beach
in the suburbs
a girl sits and cries.
The waves hear an echo
of unborn emotions,
unrealized mountains
and ungiven gifts.
The wind brings
a shiver that
travels the waters
only to be felt
by those who
hear the call.

Nobody

nobody
walks this painted line
desperately balancing
a grocery list of pain.
nobody
looks into the room
after switching off
the lamp
to see a streak of moon
on her hair.
nobody
listens to the melody
coming from the kitchen
while she dances
with her baby
as dinner boils on
the stove.
nobody
shivers with a chill
as a breeze tries
to invade.
nobody
can take her steps
and soften the concrete.
nobody
is always by her side.

Getting Through

The hard days
more frequent,
tipping the scale
from the balance
I have fumbled.
Faces look for
guidance at what
expression to hold.
Movements are slow
as the days pass
in an instant
of validity.
Straining against
the fence.
Composure unstable.
Finding a crack,
I crawl through.

War Zone

Hang my face at the door,
replace it with
a protective coating
guaranteed to shield me
from elementary anguish.
My movements are careful
trying to avoid the careless bombs
detonating in my path.
Blue bursts of fire
hurled in my direction
cause me to duck,
run, hide inside myself
for fear of abusive mines
laid in my path.

So Far Away

In a day that seems
to have dimmers on
for the rising fog clouds,
warm hands guide
your way.
With a kindred spirit
creating guardian angels
has become the way
to surround you
in my love.
Low, humming vibrations
reach their
destination and
send their replies.
Sparks shoot out
from the words.
A warm rain
starts falling.

Unneeded

I guess I just don't understand
Why it has to be this way.
Silent.
Brooding.
Just do.
No questions.
So here I am.
Explaining to me why I wonder
when I get to be the one.
The one who rants,
the one who orders,
the one who storms.
So I quietly wring my hands
for being unneeded;
furniture to rest your feet
then walk away.

Disappointing Breeze

I can feel it
with each subtle
flutter of the wind.
I am hesitant to move
as the sensations
are skeptical
of my ability to
move the right way.
I sit so still
I can feel the
softness of my eyelashes
as the breeze
teases the tips.
My heart is heavy today,
leaden with
unsophistication and
longing for contentment.

Hypnotized

You have changed me again.
I travel down a different hallway,
heart leading,
beating overwhelming emotion.
A hand reaches out-
a startling sting on my cheek
that knocks me to the floor.
The cool linoleum
recognizes the burn.
With my back against the wall,
I rewind the cinematic moments
inserting your verbal roadblock
and pieces fall away
to reveal a puzzle
much more simple than its shell.
Easier to dissect
if we try.

Another Door

Pacing the room,
making treads,
feeling low.
Waves of realization
over what is happening
grab at me with
punchy fingers.
The static gets louder
the outline fuzzier.
The door opens and
I know I must step through.
Leaving behind one room
to enter another.
I lock the door
temporarily knowing
I can return.
Knowing I might not
be allowed back in.
I sit alone
without windows,
without comfort,
save for the voice
in my head that tells me
to remain for awhile.

Living in My House

The beginning stanza
is always the same-
a realization has struck
and cleared the way
for a thought or two.
You may never see it my way.
You may never understand why I cry.
You may never walk beside me
without a condescending hand
to point out the missteps and stumbles.
I may never explain why
I look out the window
and see the mountains as a haven.
You don't understand my muse.
You blur at my verse
and throw it aside
telling me its not worth a dime.
Could you remember one phrase?
One soulful line from
the dozens of papers left for you
on the nightstand.
The frames look silly to me now.
Jumbled in a heap on the floor.
Lost kittens that no one ever
took the chance to love.
I cradle them in my arms
and search for the words
to soothe them back into existence.
You may never understand why
the door closed behind me
and the hallway was still.

I Don't Have the Strength

Don't have the strength to be fair.
Don't have the strength to stop.
Don't have the strength to erase this.
After tumbling down a mountain
of thorns in a home with cold walls,
my own stupidity clocks me
in the head with each trigger.
Don't have the strength to shut up.
Don't have the strength to sit down.
Don't have the strength to hold back.
Tripping over my own tongue,
I gather the sticks for my nest.
I know I will send for a sign,
dance by the fire,
enjoy hallucinations created
from the smoke.
Don't have the strength to submit.
Don't have the strength to comply.
Don't have the strength to fade.

Naked

The forgotten art
of selflessness
lies within the argument
we had today.
I think back to
my mirror image
and the frosted
white eye shadow.
The creamy powder was
going to make you
love me forever.
Transforming brown eyes
into stars.
And when I cried, it ran.
My swollen lids
betrayed me,
stripped me away
from my ego.
I've misplaced the charade.
I have forgotten my lines.
Exit stage right.
I enter your arms
and reveal my identity.

Flashes of Red

In My Head

Floating, almost giddy,
impossibly sexy and strong.
The physical vacillates from
impatient to enjoyment of
fantasies created.
The emotional pushes
towards genuine affection
then disbelief.
So much bubbling
under my skin.
Flowing lava pooling
into the soft, cool
area behind my ear.
Waiting.
A humming fills
my head.
Growing louder and louder
as I sink backward
into the bed.
The lava starts to drain
into my blood and travel
down my spine.
The heat reaches
each tip of my fingers
and I cannot maintain
the silence.

Sex

I am addicted
to the smell
taste
touch
scratching and clawing
for a morsel
of sex
love
wet
stretching my body
for sun
light
faith
Grabbing a hold
of hard
soft
heat.

Bonfire

The fire is back.
A soggy paper napkin
ignited with much wringing
and stroking.
A small spark
turned into a bonfire
to light the night sky.
A blaze of passion
stoked by trust and truth.
Leaving icy cold mornings
in the past
and starting each day
with an inferno.

Entranced

Entranced.
Enraptured.
Captivated.
Mesmerized.
The ideas float
as filmy curtains
blow on a light wind.
Soft, overstuffed pillows
surround our heads.
Our outlines form
shadows on the wall
as the evening light
turns to a dusky rose.
My foot investigates
your toes as our
hushed tones fill
the room with an
easy murmur.
Warm lips.
Sweetness flows
as the buzzing continues
inside my head.
Heated skin.
Our movements smooth
on the sheets.
Sensuous.
Fluid.
Sumptuous.
Lush.

Senses

You can see it.
Beaming from
my eyes,
dripping from
my fingertips
as they lazily
graze your cheek.
You can feel it.
A history of
mismatched lovers.
Useful,
but non-foretelling
of this one.
A great love
to encompass
my senses.
A smooth,
twisting track
leaving me breathless.
You can taste it.
On my tongue
as we kiss.
The grandeur
of sticky, sweet love.
You will know it.
Waking to my
warm, sweaty form
or dipping biscotti into
frothy brew at our

kitchen table.
Finding our way
along the wall
using only our senses.

Yin Yang

On the
surface
the separation
is apparent.
The dark
on light never
intruding on
the other.
peer closer-
a revelation
of swirling
emulsion
of love,
sex and
discovery of self.
It is a
never ending
pursuit to become
the other
while retaining
the luminous
white
and deep, onyx black.

My Reality

Your concerns
lead my thoughts
to grip my words.
Have I spoken my heart?
Daylight exists
as a revelation
when you throw a sleepy arm
over and pull me in.
Here lies a crystal wall
of flowing emotion
dripping from unforeseen
flashes of ecstasy.
Memories created
by the mere fact
that we fit.
This compilation denotes
the sweetest taste
on the very tip of my tongue.
The smoothest movement
of this dance we've joined.
Through the haze,
I touch your face
and then you know.

Goodnight

I feel you before
you enter.
I hear your steps as they
approach,
The click of the door,
the smell of your shirt,
it's a comfort to be savored
every night.
It's a sigh of relief to be
reunited
in our favorite place
In the dark,
I growl.
Sometimes,
I moan.
Usually,
I snore,
but my heart swells
at your sounds,
your clattering about.
I cannot lay my head
deep into night
until you are wrapped
around me and your
rhythm matches mine.

Lord, Help Me

Lord help me I'm falling.
Into a big white pillow
soft and sexy
filled with the heat
of my lover.
He surrounds my body
with surprising intensity
as the sounds of the city
beat sporadic outside my window.
Lord, help me I'm falling
into a self induced
conceptual maze of excitement.
He brings me to various
levels of heat.
He fills my blood,
makes me complete.
Lord, help me I've fallen
and I don't want to land.
Bring me back to this place
I want to see his face
in the pillow on my bed.

Creamy White

Theirs

I bear witness to this love.
The swirling evolvement that
bubbles and rolls like morning tea.
It started in a way familiar to all of us.
Young, curious, almost silently growing
within their hands
as if they held their hearts in their
palms and it was beating hard the
intensity they now display.
A vibrant woman picks flowers of independence.
A genuine man ticking away at complexity.
This love has held many weights
of various measures.
The sinewy fibers stretched over oceans,
a flaming trail from his heart to hers.
Although my words cannot mold
this masterpiece or foretell
the future with this technicolor narrative,
I bear witness to this love
because of its purity and honor.
I am a better soul
to be present.

Waiting for Grace

Waiting for you
questions swirl
around independent subjects.
Time crawls after
squeezing into a second.
No one can know
the thoughts heavy
in your frame.
No one can know
the profound weight
I experience each moment.
The pod I carry
combines our spirits
and on the outside
we are separated by fear.
So close to feeling what
I know we will feel.
So close to having
sweetness indescribable by any.
But our backs touch
in the same place we
created her.
Silence I understand.
Brooding I try to comfort.
Panic I share only with you.
As husband and wife we
communicate without words.
As man and woman
the mysteries abound.
Money sex security
happiness peace comfort
time truth lust.

Our Wedding

The sun goes down
upon the birth of our day.
Crystal reflections
portray the balance
of perfection and
destiny.
Visions of this day
dance with anticipation
united with the ritual tears
of ultimate emotion.
The golden gauntlet
thrown by our parents,
vibrates with tradition
and the infinite.
Love has become
the theme.
Marriage the subtitle.
the story is yet unwritten,
but the ending
is a celebration
of the union
of two souls determined
to survive.

The Promise

That time will
forever stop
when you walk
into the room.
That trust
unspoken is
the foundation
of our lives.
That passion
will breathe
and sigh
as we grow.
That tragedy
will bring the
comfort of
my arms.
That every
secret is
kept
and lies
never create.
That our vows
are the ones
we make ever day.
that in death
only then
will our bodies
be apart
and our souls
fly away.

Leo

A piece of my heart
separated from
its home inside my chest
traveled south to
nestle itself inside my womb.
My flesh heaved out
a fully formed
technically functional
emotional and real
human being.
My chin,
his nose
soft, sweet hair,
searching eyes
that ask questions
only I understand.

Saffron

Serenity

Serenity would be
waking with the curtains drawn
windows open.
A knock at the door
presents
coffee, bacon, red strawberries,
bits of sweet
bits of salty.
Opening the curtain
you roll over and smile
a sleepy grin
realizing
I am still here.

It's Just the Way You Are

You would never think
of letting me go without a word.
Sideways glances told me
that you understood.
That girl who stopped us understood.
Its just the way you are.
You always manage
to tell me the right things
at the right times
with the right caress of your voice.
Its just the way you are.
You couldn't fathom the idea
of jumping up to get a towel,
instead you sigh in my ear
and throw a leg over mine.
Our bodies still tingling,
eyes still half closed.
Its just the way you are.
After years of grabbing each other
by the collar
through a dull, gray monitor
when one of us was floundering,
you reach in and pull me to the surface,
brush me off, kiss me behind my ear,
and tell me you love me.
Its just the way you are.
And the way you are
is the way I want it to be.

But I Can

Baby, you are so far away.
I can't rock you to sleep.
I can't make your coffee in the morning.
I can't smile at you over my shoulder
or warm your towel on the heater.
I can't squeeze your hand in traffic,
buy you small gifts just because.
But I can believe.
I can smile walking through the mall,
remembering a moment.
I can listen. Really listen.
I can open up my heart
to so many senses never discovered.
I can try and tell you the impression
you have left from the heat of
your hands and the images
your words create.
I can tell you the truth
as it comes to my heart
and know that you understand.
I can be with you sometimes
and love you always.
I can't be next to you most times.
But I can be close to you as
high as the sky goes.

In Your Head

Your own
truth
is mirrored in
her eyes.
reasons exist
for the
solid connection.
Unexplainable
by choice,
endurance
inevitable.
Parallel thoughts
without words,
merely a voice
in her head.
Comfort surrounds
me constantly.
From beginning
to end
it will
be ours.

Sail With Me

I have chosen
a different path.
One that leads to
tributaries foreign
to the comforts I
have built.
The colors seem deeper,
the emotion stronger.
I have come to rely
on the adventure,
the challenge to
find a new branch,
dangle my feet
in the silky, cool water.
Because it's different
than the warm bath
drawn at home.
I peer down
at my own reflection
and I see the glitter
that had once faded.

It's You

A giddy light
ridiculous in its brightness
revealing the truth
yet never releasing
its unwavering intensity.
It guides me through
the darkest corners
of my soul.
It holds the water
in its hands
for me to drink.
It caresses my head
when the world has
shut down and gone home.
The light, as it is,
is not symbolic.
Its human form
sheds a shadow
over me
and occupies every
thought of eternity.
The light in its purest form
is you.

In an Instant

Nothing can prepare you
for the life,
the instant joy and dread,
the exhilaration and exhaustion
of motherhood.
You feel beautiful
and hideous,
powerful and inadequate,
strength and depth in
a time where no mother
feels she can stumble.
Months go by and
the creases smooth
into sheets of fresh
smelling laundry and
bananas.

My Joy

One on my arm
another in my purse
looking for a quarter.
Juggling juice.
Pleading for an arm
to slide easily into
a winter jacket.
No you cannot have
more stickers.
Yes I do have your
binky in my pocket.
Hold my hand.
Don't do that.
Take this.
Hold on!
Walk faster!
Please look where
you are going!
Sigh.
Made it into the car.

Beiges and Browns

Ecosystem

My ecosystem has been
altered to contain two
weighted environments.
One is Spring.
A new flower budding
and covered in dew.
I cradle her and cherish
the blossoming.
I nourish the earth
occasionally running
from the lightening and thunder.
The other is Fall.
Scarlet leaves and
glowing embers of a
dancing fire.
Left alone most of the time
to grow and feed off
of its own momentum.
I am split between them
and walk each field
in my mind every day.
I tend to each of the gardens
and I run through the tall,
sweet grass and
treasure every moment.
The sun is warm
and I know that
I don't have to choose.
I can pick the flowers
and watch the leaves turn
merely by shifting my gaze.

Disengaged

Time transforms,
and has clocks whirling.
Amoebic souls
struggle to understand
why it was,
how it isn't
why I felt
and now I don't.
Lush, moist forest
turns to barren desert.
Love turns to confusion.
Slowly becoming something
so twisted and gnarled.
Pain turns to
strange freedom,
warm lightness,
cool independence.
Change becomes
a friend.

Building a Home

As I sit in the corner knees up
contemplating the room
I gather strength from the door.
The welcoming handle leads me
to a strange, yet brilliantly
sunny place of freedom.
I have opened it
and stepped through
only to return to my corner
to contemplate the room.
I own this room.
I own everything in it
including the pride
that came creating it.
But there are cracks,
cracks in the foundation
that cannot be repaired.
On one journey,
I found a new dwelling.
A dazzling, yet comfortable multi level,
solid home.
And every day
I dream of the day
when I can decorate it
and caress its walls
to find the true beauty
it so richly deserves.
Until then,
I sit in the corner
and contemplate the room.

Distraction

Walking, strolling
with one
then another
mind here
thoughts there
Sounds of traffic
honking
invading
momentarily bringing
me to front and center.
Emotions only comparable
to my daughter laughing.
Wandering lost
in my walking dreams.
Aching
needing
accepting the script as written.
I cross the street
hail a cab
and my mind never wanders
from you.

Time

A shadow slides
towards the wall
and slinks through the
cracks before I can
grasp it
step on it
stop it from passing
through my room
like a cat burglar
with no other
purpose than to
steal a glance at your
bedspread pattern.
The shadow leaves
behind more darkness.
Under my eyes,
under my behind,
in the yard
beside the trees.
Yesterday,
I made a snowman.
With tingling fingers,
snowballs became
light
and the shadows ceased
to visit.

Marathon

It becomes all encompassing
to imagine freedom.
The mind surges with
the crazy laughter of
a naked man
running the streets
with a torch lit
for eternity.
The symbolic spirit
of the rebellious soul.
Red bombs explode
in his head with each step,
mines threaten to
remove any trace
of this isolated
sprint to the finish line.
Peace holds real value
with each cold slap
of the soles of his
weathered feet.
The sun indicates another
cold nightfall ahead
as dusk settles and the crowds
go home for meatloaf
and mashed potatoes.
His eyes begin to water
as the wind blows colder
and just as he begins to slow,
a figure appears under

a street lamp ahead.
The hazy figure reveals
an outstretched hand
starting to run.
The man reaches her
and thrusts the torch
into her hand
just as he collapses
to the ground
face down in the dust.
The naked woman
continues the journey.
Destiny brought her to this place.
Her belief in equality
carries her legs and
warms her blood.
One hundred miles away
a man waits, naked,
yet filled with purpose

Bath

The water has reached
my constricted throat.
Gently rising
with intent to take
the breath from
my selfless lips.
My fingers reach.
My legs flail for stability.
The icy flow
has turned my velvet
skin blue,
joints aching,
thoughts still.
Another millimeter
another desperate prayer
to stop the vice on my heart.
I flip the knob.
the water drains and
twists my fears
as they slowly disappear.

Examination

I am restless with itchy
fingers.
I cannot decide what
to paint,
what to sculpt,
what to mold into a
perfect slice of my sanity.
Each day I reach for
that color that
speaks to me.
A sumptuous velvet red
or floral lime green
picked out of a painting
created by a local artist
hanging at Starbucks.
Its also an emptiness,
a longing I know
deep within that
will remain until
I finish something.

The Mountain

My breath.
I can't seem to find it,
hold it.
The haze surrounding
the street lamps
prelude the collapse
of my lungs.
I reach for your hand
and the dizziness
fills my eyes with
foggy, filtered steam.
Tears sting as my
breathing gains strength.
There is no bridge
to cross over.
There is a mountain
to climb.

Standing Outside

Somewhere
I can see you.
A bit dim,
but a sweet
shadow
inside a room
filled with
happiness and
promise.
I am not
ready to enter.
I will knock.

For You

I'll take the hard
and the wretched,
the haste
and the affliction.
I'll take the petty
and the ignorant
to have one moment
in your arms.
I'll take no sleep,
long days
and a tired head
to discuss our life
deep into the night.
I need to look
into those eyes
to see the love
we have nurtured
like a child
with a gentle touch
and a kiss.
My lips are
a promise only
to you.
With every glance
I fall deeper
into you.
With each day
I am true to
what I know

to be true love.
I'll take what
needs to be
to be with you
forever.

Shades of Gray

Chasing the Light

In a hazy dream
I walked towards a
luminous warmth.
My feet seemed to float.
My mind flew
with the birds above.
Patches of sun
broke into shards
and gave me choices
as to which line
to follow.
Slowly as my
body returned to the ground
my heart began to thud
with a heavy new beat.
Longing to find my way,
the light was skipping
ahead beckoning me
with its fingers.
I start to run
as the light eludes my eyes.
I stop to sit
and wonder why I am
chasing the light.

The Anatomy of Needing

The anatomy of needing
includes a starvation diet
while floating delicacies
underneath my nose,
waft their scent,
tease my mouth,
tempt my bones.
The make up of a woman
programmed for life
is to want more,
dream about more
following the smoky trail
of needing more.
The summation that
follows gluttony
includes an inventory
of what was there
is not right now.
Need births more need.
A conception that begins
from a passionate truth,
feeding my lips
dripping in desire.

Awaken

Pieces of me
have left
in search of a
different answer.
Chromatic dreams
awake me with a start
and reveal
that I am not whole,
will not be whole,
until I gather
the information my soul
begs for.
For the first time
I know
love is not the answer.

Secrets

Nobody knows everything.
Speeches and confessions
fighting to escape.
Daily faces hang behind
the bathroom door,
masks that complete
the present condition.
Painted in the garage,
fumes gagging,
thick, oily liquid dripping
creating a mosaic on the floor.
An ironic mix of several lives
combined to form happiness.

Day Dreaming

In one mind
the swirls,
the infinite palate
of time faces each one.
Bizarre in a sense
funky to a degree
of contemplation.
Deep, soothing
theater of the perspective.
Elaborate costumes
gold, encrusted jewels.
The moment passes
and I blink my eyes.

Strange Existence

A silent vow
only heard by my heart
a promise not to flee
seems ridiculous at times
through a strange door at night
cold sheets
warm shower
rising to the pact we made
absence of tenure
moving to the music
hearing a different song
inside my head
dancing lightly
as my gaze falls down
to my hands.

Waiting

What am I doing?
Waiting. Just quietly
waiting for you to fit
the pieces of your life's
puzzle together and to
find out if I have a
corner or a center piece
or none at all.
Days, months, years
fly and we got caught
in the wind with our wings
out, but now it seems
its not enough to fly
or love or laugh.
I am auditioning for a part
in your future
to which the script
has not been written.
Please, give me a hint
because I tire going
home not knowing
if I'll get the lead
or if the curtain will
fall as fast as it went up.
I'm hesitant of my own
moves and I ache to
ask you what I should do
what we should do.
What I should do.

Breaking the Cycle

All around me is weights,
weakness learned,
habits to break.
So much frustration of mind,
power crackling that
I've yet to find.
Cover your eyes, dear,
embrace the old.
The fear is gone.
The cocoon will shatter and
bold, exotic wings emerge.
Inside me
every hypnotic surge
pressing over the tops
of the highest trees
to reach my goal

18

Sometimes
it hits me
at the strangest
of moments.
A sad realization
that people
are complex
and distracted.
Some are unsatisfied
by the gifts they
fail to realize
that are set
before them
on a platter lined with
golden promise
of a successful and
contented life.
Others are ignorant.
I tell myself that
because I fail to
believe the
cruelty of abuse
doled out by hand
or spat by the lips
of an insecure child
laced with infinite
moments of damage and guilt.
I try to be
the nurturer.

A mother of sorts
who cradles the strays,
comforts the broken,
or cries alone
after witnessing
such horrors.
But, like them,
I am alone.
The pain I feel
is for them.
Betrayed by my own heart.
I am wrought
at not knowing my role.
Not knowing how to help.
A blessing and a gift.

Changing Hues

Soul Sister

The ebb and flow
of our spirits
become a
foundation for
the awakening.
Constant movement
belies the bubbling
lava we contain.
Dancing around
the fire,
we scream our
freedom and battle the
demons flung
in our path.
Holding hands
the sparks
kiss our backs,
the brush
scratches our feet
bloody and raw.
The moon smiles
and lights
our way to morning.

First Steps

The mystical,
spell that wrapped
my thoughts
with a thick, sticky
webbing
dissolved into the
cool, Autumn air.
The slow, magnetic force
draws me to the spiritual
height that is my
ultimate goal.
The moon hovers,
watching over
the newborn
taking her first
shaky steps.
One after another
leading me to God.

Psychic Thoughts

Your own
truth
mirrored in
her eyes.
Reasons exist
for the
solid connection,
unexplainable
by choice
endurance inevitable.
Parallel thoughts
without words
merely a voice
in my head.
Comfort surrounds
me constantly.
From beginning
to end,
it will be ours.

Lying in Bed

In the silence
the air sparks
and I know.
The phone doesn't ring
but the messages
in my head
keep coming along the wire.
Staring at the ceiling
I am surrounded
by the warm blanket
woven by your thoughts.
The need is immense at times
the urge to connect
grows with each
second I breathe.
I look into the fire
and the flames
act out my desire.
I know you are there.
in my head.
In my heart.
In the silence.

Sensibility

Sensibility intrudes and
bursts into the room
when absurdity had
occupied the floor.
I prefer to scramble
through ecstasy rather
than amble through
distraction.
I find myself
trapped in dark caves
inside my head after
following a path
I knew was merely a habit
rather than a desire.
My intention grows as
my passions go unfulfilled
where I reside.
Pinpoints of light
guide me toward what
can be interpreted
as altruistic in the real world.
I am seeking the
hot sun flooding
the room with satisfaction.

Quilt

The words we say
are woven with
choices
tossed over
all night long.
You stare
at the ceiling
and make decisions
on what truly
exists.
Integrity behind
closed doors.
Introducing yourself
to you.
The clean beginning
of ignorance when
casual conversation
breathe as hard facts.
Surrender the blanket
and acquire another
piece.

Time to Rest

Creating organic filters
to wade through the muck
I admit stagnation
is not an option.
I come to a clearing
and rest on a bed of rock.
A sensation washes over
my body and I know
you are thinking of me.
The cosmic connection
is a constant reminder
of the possibilities
fragmented by our separation.
Looking to the sky,
I am truly grateful for
this attachment
as I know that as long
as I breathe it will be.

Innocence

I was
a child once.
Wide eyed,
ever trusting,
skinning my knees
on the gravel out back
as I battled the imagined
bad guys.
Understanding more than
I knew.
Terrified at what was
becoming clear.
I didn't want the
secrets of the world.
Bloody knees
melted inward,
and hurt
began to hurt.
Old Man Time
hurled my emotions
into the future
and I climbed into
Daddy's lap,
rocking slowly,
feeling nothing.

Makeupping

Puffy lids and pasty tongue
fail to present an obvious
tidbit of anticipation.
Tackle box of rainbow
pretension lands on the
sink bed with a thump.
Clasps click and brushes
drag across protruding bone.
Amidst the flying powder
and dripping clay
this canvas is responding
surprisingly well to the attack.
But faith exists beneath the
semi-confident strokes and blotting.
The belief that one out of
every 7 days, a smudge
and a swipe will bring up the sun
and force one to dig out those
strappy, black sandals almost
too daring for the office,
unheard of in the checkout aisle,
but the flawless accessory needed
to complete this showpiece.
A quick glance in the hall mirror
and you realize the sparkling
light coming through is
from within.
Not from a bottle.

A Sign

Please deliver to me
a sign.
It can be love.
It can be malice.
No matter.
Forgive me for longing
to be guided.
The spirits are around me
I am sure.
I'm not sure just where
or when or why.
A full moon makes me ponder.
Am I alone?
Is this reality?
Do I have the power?
This is the knowledge
I need.
A clap of thunder,
a whisper in my ear.
Give me the secret.
I want peace from knowledge.
With enlightenment comes pain.
Pain is a relief.
Curiosity is the trigger.

First Breath

It has never been
a reality that
has not caused
pain from the pressure
of performance.
Until a sunrise created
the perfect day,
the molding of time
with fingers of fire.
A gentle smoothing
of heart creases.
It begins with a kiss
and ends with the
warmth of my
beloved's heartbeat.

His God Within

He lay drenched at my feet, hands bleeding.
Pulling my fingers to his lips, crying, "Why? Why?"
He needed so much to know what it was
he answered to, dreamt about, felt so
incessantly in his heart was true.
Centuries ago, yet he lives for salvation
and he waits for signs of it.
Forever haunted by nature's demons,
powers not to be controlled
only made worse with each sin.
The golden lights are the pathway
to another time which had borne his soul,
aching for a presence to heal
the scars of bondage-
freedom from pain.

He Wasn't the One

The scent of an
old, familiar friend
comes over me.
A choice I didn't make
but don't regret
but still ponder
a different life.
Not my house
or even my town.
Strange holidays
for different anniversaries.
Maybe a better checkbook balance.
Maybe not.
Possibly more arguments
or incompatible sex.
My mind drifts as I drive by
the house and then
the images disappear
as I look in my rearview mirror
and see the angelic face
of my sleeping child.

978-0-595-67028-4
0-595-67028-8

Printed in the United States
135381LV00002B/19/A